Space Fox is Wild Bird's pal.
But Wild Bird must go home.

2 Space Fox will take Wild Bird home.
They get in Space Fox's space ship.

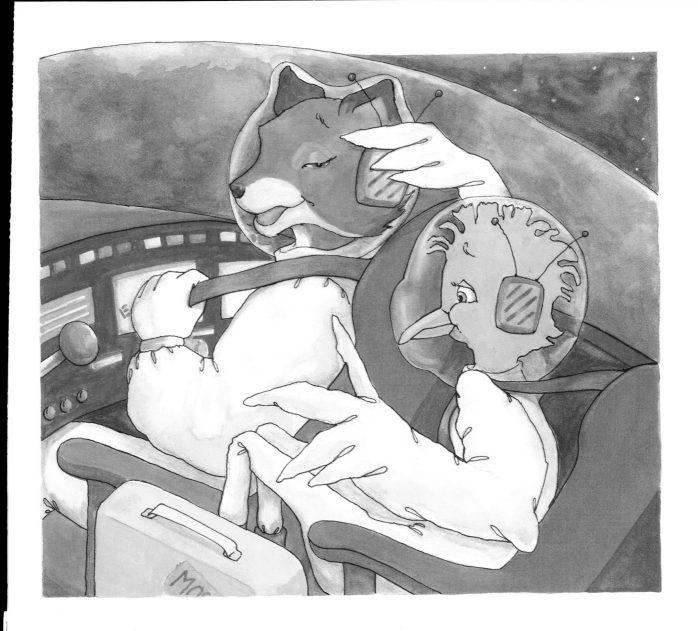

It will take a lot of time.
"I will take a nap," said Space Fox.
"Please do not be a pest Wild Bird."

3

4

Wild Bird sneaks past Space Fox.
Wild Bird pulls on the rod.

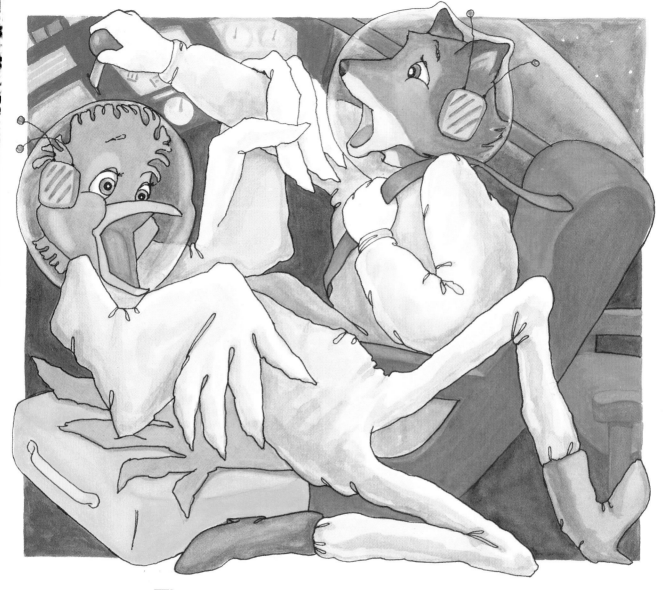

The space ship spins fast.
Space Fox blinks and jumps up.
"Stop, stop!" yells Space Fox.
Wild Bird yells, "Help!"

5

6

But Space Fox can not stop it.
They run out of gas.

At last, the space ship rests on a nest.
It is Wild Bird's nest.

7

8

"Home, sweet home," says Wild Bird.
"Yes," says Space Fox.
"But next time, we will take the space bus!"